Law of Attraction

----- ◈◈◈ -----

The 9 Most Important Secrets to Successfully Manifest Health, Wealth, Abundance, Happiness and Love

Ryan James

Table of Contents

Introduction 1

Chapter 1- How the law of attraction works 5

Chapter 2: Attracting Love 15

Chapter 3: Attracting Wealth 21

Chapter 4: Attracting Health 27

Chapter 5: The Ultimate Goal: Abundance and Happiness 35

Closing 41

© Copyright 2016 by Ryan James - All rights reserved.

This document is geared towards providing exact and reliable information in regards to the topic and issue covered. The publication is sold with the idea that the publisher is not required to render accounting, officially permitted, or otherwise, qualified services. If advice is necessary, legal or professional, a practiced individual in the profession should be ordered.

- From a Declaration of Principles which was accepted and approved equally by a Committee of the American Bar Association and a Committee of Publishers and Associations.

In no way is it legal to reproduce, duplicate, or transmit any part of this document in either electronic means or in printed format. Recording of this publication is strictly prohibited and any storage of this document is not allowed unless with written permission from the publisher. All rights reserved.

The information provided herein is stated to be truthful and consistent, in that any liability, in terms of inattention or otherwise, by any usage or abuse of any policies, processes, or directions contained within is the solitary and utter responsibility of the recipient reader. Under no circumstances will any legal responsibility or blame be held against the publisher for any reparation, damages, or monetary loss due to the information herein, either directly or indirectly.

Respective authors own all copyrights not held by the publisher.

The information herein is offered for informational purposes solely, and is universal as so. The presentation of the information is without contract or any type of guarantee assurance.

The trademarks that are used are without any consent, and the publication of the trademark is without permission or backing by the trademark owner. All trademarks and brands within this book are for clarifying purposes only and are the owned by the owners themselves, not affiliated with this document.

Introduction

"Be careful what you wish for, it may just come true". We've all heard the saying and it only goes to show that although *the law of attraction* may be a new concept, it is not a new idea. Philosophers have pondered about it for hundreds of years, stressing the importance of positive attitude and optimistic take on life.

The power of mind is, actually, scary. For those who know how to use it (for positive or negative reasons) it is the ultimate tool of creation or destruction.

It has now been scientifically proven that our thoughts, especially if we've been having them for a long time, or if they'd been instilled in our mind by someone else, eventually get accepted as facts, and as such, usually turn into reality.

This happens because both our thoughts and words project into the universe from where they return to us as manifestations, i.e. we attract what we think about.

Introduction

The sad thing is that, according to psychologists, most of our thoughts are negative. This, perhaps, is not surprising considering the current state of the world – economic and political crisis, natural disasters and constant threat of nuclear annihilation.

However, it's also true that the thoughts we have, whether because of low self-esteem or because we've been brainwashed that we are not good enough for certain things in life, usually become a part of our blueprint, and as such, are very difficult to get rid of.

There are those who claim that no matter how hard, or how long, they tried to change their lives with the help of the law of attraction principles, nothing happened. This is because making a wish come true is not a straightforward process.

Whether you'll get what you ask for depends on many things, including on where you're coming from. Just like looking for a job after you've been laid off puts you in a disadvantaged position when negotiating your pay, hoping to attract love, wealth or happiness at a time when you are going through a personal crisis (e.g. divorce, loss of income, health problems, etc.) makes it more difficult to work.

Law of Attraction

If you feel overwhelmed with unhappiness, loneliness or some other kind of desperation, it's better to first try and sort out your life and once the worst is over, you can calmly, and without urging desperation, focus your attention on the changes you want in your life.

The law of attraction, if used properly, can change our life for the better, by allowing us to live our dreams.

The key thing with the law of attraction is that we have the ability to attract the things we want in life, and the trick is to learn the art of using the law of attraction to our advantage.

Since visualization is the key element of the law of attraction, just spending 20 minutes a day visualizing that which we want to manifest in our lives, can significantly help us in getting it. Obviously just hoping and dreaming will get us nowhere if we don't act, but it can inspire us. And inspiration is a positive driver for success.

It's a well-known fact that champion athletes directly influence their physical abilities by spending time on creative visualization. This means that "seeing" yourself succeed in something (getting a job, finding a relationship, creating wealth, etc) you are already half way

Introduction

there. But, don't just visualize your results, EXPECT results.

Equally, feeling sorry for yourself, being full of self-doubt or negativity undermines your confidence and kills your enthusiasm, leading to more negative thoughts, which attracts more self-doubt, and on and on...to a never ending down ward spiral. The key is to start an upward spiral of positive thoughts instead of a negative one.

Free-Gift- Grab your copy of the free E-book at http://bit.ly/subtlepsychology

Chapter 1-

How the law of attraction works

The idea of the law of attraction is actually very simple and it makes a lot of sense – you attract what you think about.

Believing that you deserve better or more, you usually end up getting what you think you deserve. Or, if you believe strongly that you will get cured, the chances of getting cured increase greatly.

However, we must remember that not everything works for everyone, and just like one type of medication will heal one person but not the other, the law of attraction is about harnessing the power of the universe in fulfilling our dreams. By learning how to use this power properly, you will greatly increase the chances of it working for you.

Chapter 1- How the law of attraction works

Put simply, there's not much point boosting your morale with affirmations, positive thinking or the like if deep down (and that's the most powerful part of your mind) you "know" you're not going to get healed, or get the job, or whatever.

Repeating positive affirmations like mantras, while being full of doubt and gloom is a waste of time and can only lead to disappointment. You need to really believe that your life can change, that there is still hope, or that you will eventually be healed.

Although techniques for attracting love into your life may differ from those you will use if you want to attract wealth, there are some general guidelines for manifesting one's dreams. You don't need any special training or skills, although spiritually sensitive people will find it easier to tune-in with the unseen forces of the universe.

Here are 9 secrets for successful tuning-in with the universal law of attraction:

1. <u>Know what you want and why you want it.</u>

   Sometimes despite all our efforts our wishes don't come true, simply because they are not "right" for us at the time. They say there's something like "divine timing", meaning you get what you need not when you ask for it, but when the universe thinks you are ready for it.

However, many people feel they want a change in their life, but are not sure what exactly that change should be. If you feel something's missing in your life, but don't know what it is, you have probably become disconnected with your inner wisdom. Something, or someone, is holding you back and you need to get that out of the way in order to manifest your heart's desire.

You can manifest all that you want by believing what you want is possible and feeling confident you will get it.

There are different resources and practices that can help you get clarity about your true desires, but the two easiest methods are asking yourself where your true passion lies or writing about it. Write down whatever comes from your heart. You'll be surprised how much your heart has to tell you if you only cared to listen.

Chapter 1- How the law of attraction works

2. <u>Don't give up on your dreams</u>

   Don't be ashamed or afraid of your dreams, even if most people will laugh at you. Those who won't accept you for what you are, or in whose company you, for whatever reason feel uncomfortable, need to be removed from your life. If your environment is not supportive of what you do, remember that people often do that out of envy, because they didn't have the courage to pursue their dreams. Knowing what you are will make it much easier working out what you need most in life. Say NO to life of pretence even if it will lose you a few friends. Being true to yourself raises your vibrations and makes it easier to focus on what you really want in life.

3. <u>Ask yourself why you haven't been able to have the things that you now need so badly.</u>

   You need to be brutally honest with yourself, as more often than not it is our own bad choices, unrealistic expectations or insufficient willpower that led us into lives we now have to live. Rather than blaming others for unfulfilled dreams, think how you would do things differently if you had a second chance.

We rarely get things right the first time. Getting a second chance in life is about giving yourself the opportunity to grow beyond your past failures.

So what if your life is a mess? First acknowledge the mistake you made, take the blame, learn from it, then move on. Don't dwell on past for years - too much self-analysis is not healthy.

Admitting to yourself you were wrong is hard, but sometimes we learn more from the painful experiences that we would have if everything had gone according to plan.

4. <u>What if nothing works for you?</u>

If despite all your efforts you haven't been able to get any of your wishes come true, then it's probably a case of bad energy. Different cultures deal with the problem of negative energy in different ways: the Chinese would clear the energy of their living or working space with Feng Shui, Indians would offer prayers and offerings,

Chapter 1- How the law of attraction works

some would start going to church, others may try working harder, etc

Practice whatever you feel comfortable with. Negative energy can come from different sources and there are many ways of increasing both your personal energy and the energy of your environment.

5. <u>Raise your vibrations.</u>

    Before attempting to "communicate" with the universe, you need to raise your vibrations. You can do this by cleansing your body and mind of toxic thoughts, people and habits, thus gradually tuning-in into the more positive way of thinking and being.

    De-clutter your life from people who drain you of energy. Create more "breathing space" by ending shallow friendships. "Unfollow" your contacts on social media that doesn't add value to your life and surround yourself with like-minded people in whose company you feel safe and comfortable.

6. <u>Be patient</u>

   Don't expect success to manifest within days (although it might). If your life, or environment, had been filled with negativity, anger, sadness or similar destructive emotions, it may take some time for your personal "energy field" to clear, soften and become more receptive of positive vibrations.

   Depression or long illness depletes us of emotional and spiritual energy, making it difficult to manifest a dream since law of attraction requires we put energy behind our intentions. If you feel your energy is very low, rather than waste time trying over and over again to manifest an intention, first try to boost your personal energy through healthy and positive living habits: healthy diet, exercise, meditation and a positive mindset.

7. <u>Focus</u>

   If you are new to the law of attraction, it's better to focus on one intention at a time. That way it'll be easier to direct and channel your thoughts where you need them to go. Focus on your intention and stay with it. Remind yourself of it at least once a day, maybe first thing in the morning or just before going to bed. As you think about it smile, feel positive and confident it will manifest.

8. <u>See the big picture</u>

When formulating your intention, think what it is that you really need right now. There is often a discrepancy between what we want and what we need.

For example, you may desperately want a loving relationship after a breakup, while what you actually need, may be to spend some time on your own and reflect on what you had recently gone through.

When sending out an intention to the universe, we need to know not only what we want, but why we want it. We should try and put that manifestation in perspective. Needing something badly right now, may make us happy at the moment, but maybe in the long term it could be a problem.

Sometimes, it helps to take a step back. Don't get wrapped up in sending out your intentions to the universe without ever thinking much about where you are really heading.

9. <u>Adopt a positive and open mindset</u>

    This is crucial. To manifest your dreams you need to open your heart to a new way of thinking. You have to believe that you can transform your life by replacing the negative, self-limiting thoughts with positive and empowering beliefs. Choose affirmations which best describe that which you want to manifest, and repeat them daily.

    People with a positive frame of mind think about possibilities, growth and success. They expect happiness, health, love – and they usually get it.

    They think in terms of – I CAN.

    They believe that they will accomplish what they set their mind to do. They approach even failure with a positive attitude – I'll try again.

    But, true positive thinking is not just saying that everything will be ok and secretly, dreading or even suspecting failure or problems. For your life to really

Chapter 1- How the law of attraction works

improve your positive mental attitude has to be genuine, i.e. it has to turn into a way of life.

Chapter 2:

Attracting Love

We all know that loving and being loved is very important for one's physical, mental and emotional health and with so many lonely people throughout the world, millions seem to be on the lookout for a partner.

Some people are quick to find new love, while others search for months and years, and still don't find it. How come it works for some but not for others? Are some people more loveable, or simply luckier?

Attracting love into your life has not so much to do with luck, although luck always helps, as with personal energy.

What you need to constantly remind yourself of is that you have the power to turn around your love life for the better, whether through finding a partner, improving your current relationship or being more loved and appreciated by your family and friends. But, you have to acknowledge that it is YOU who attracts or rejects opportunities.

Here are 7 tips to bear in mind when searching for love:

1. **Clarity**

    Knowing what you want always helps, as it makes is so much easier figuring out how to get it. This is particularly true when searching for love.

    Try describing your ideal partner. Not so much his/her physical looks (although if you are particular about it, why not), but their character traits. The more you go into detail, the clearer you are about what it is you really want in a partner.

2. **Prepare**

    If you have been alone for a long time, it's quite possible you've neglected yourself. If searching for love, pretend you have already met that special someone. Make sure you always (or almost always) look good - your hair, clothes, make-up. Pretend you are already dating someone.

Looking attractive and smart makes one feel good about themselves and they automatically project a more positive energy, and it is that internal energy radiating from the heart, that eventually attracts love.

3. **Focus**

When seriously searching for love you have to tune-in in the love vibration. Think often about the partner you would like to attract. Feel as if you already are in a loving relationship. Feeling loved charges our batteries and makes us project love in return. Remember the law of attraction main motto – like attracts like.

Staying focused on what you want to attract is helping you channel your energy where you want it to go. It doesn't mean you have to think about this for every waking hour of the day, but neither should you let go of the idea after a few days because you got tired.

4. **Be patient**

Don't expect your wishes to come true within days (although they might).

Chapter 2 - Attracting Love

Applying the LOA principles comes easier to some than to others and largely depends on how connected to the universe you are.

If you have generally been negative or doubtful about love, it will take longer to find someone because you first need to rewire your brain and start acting and feeling positive about yourself and your relationships. The more out of tune with love you are, the more time and effort will it take to bring you in balance with the universe.

5. **Be proactive**

   Don't stay at home, feeling lonely, unattractive and depressed, waiting to be discovered by that perfect someone. Go out, meet new people, you never know where that special person may be waiting.

   If you don't have many friends, get involved in various activities or hobbies through which you will meet new people. Psychologists agree that if for no other reason, than for the sake of our mental health, we need to do things that bring us pleasure.

6. **Love yourself**

It is unlikely to be successful in attracting anything, especially love, if you don't love yourself. And you won't be able to love yourself unless you accept yourself. Accept the way you look – if you can't be proud of your body, at least don't hate it. Respect the way your body has been serving you all these years and make a decision to start looking after it. Whatever you do don't compare yourself to celebrities. Trust me - looking glamorous takes a lot of time and tons of money.

7. **Energy**

And finally, the most important tip of all, for your intention to work, you have to put energy behind your desires. Don't do this half-heartedly. If you are unsure what kind of partner you want, or whether you want a partner at all, rather wait until you decide what it is that you want. Don't try to do this just to have someone, because everyone else does, do this only if this is what you really want. Because, unless you feel really passionate about what you want to attract, chances are it won't happen.

Chapter 3:

Attracting Wealth

They say that to attract wealth, you have to adopt a rich man's way of thinking. In other words, you have to develop a mindset of those who have already "made it".

According to a recent survey, one of the things that are typical of most rich people is that they concentrate their efforts. They identify an area, focus on it and "feed the flame".

If you believe you have what it takes to become wealthy, these are some of the principles you would have to adopt to change your mindset into a rich man's mentality:

1. **Mind power**

    Trick your mind into believing that you already have what you want. Over time, your life will change to reflect your new belief. Science has confirmed that powerful thoughts do create certain biochemical changes in the brain, which proves that rewiring your brain to adopt a rich man's mentality is possible.

2. **Pay yourself first**

Rich people do give large sums of money to charities, but they make sure their own needs are covered first. Becoming rich and staying rich means you know how to manage your wealth. Paying yourself first will help you work out what's most important in your life. In other words, prioritize and invest your money wisely. However, remember that helping those in need brings satisfaction and encourages gratitude which we all need to develop throughout life.

3. **Always think long-term**

To maintain their comfortable lifestyles, the rich constantly think of the future. Planning ahead and monitoring global political and economic developments, is how they make sure they have a future, no matter what.

4. Be proactive.

Be ready to grab an opportunity when it arises. Always be on the lookout for opportunities or challenges.

5. Be ambitious

Being ambitious is about having a clear goal of where you want to get to and a strong drive to get there. You can be ambitious without being aggressive and stepping on other people. If used wisely, ambition can get you anything you want.

6. Don't be afraid to take risks

Not everyone has the nerve to take risks, but that is something all wealthy people do, regularly or from time to time. But remember that taking calculated risks which are thought-through and managed is very different from taking foolish risks even when you don't have to.

7. Clarity

Know what you want. Have an idea of how much you want. Then go for it. Select a niche and become an expert in the field. Being clear about what and how much you

Chapter 3 - Attracting Wealth

want, will help you focus your mental and physical energy in an area you feel you can grow in.

8. Share

It's common for the rich to give money away to charities. What's interesting is that it has always been accepted as normal for the rich to give money away, not only to help those in need, but to avert bad luck.

In the past, in order to appease the Gods and ensure their continued support, the rich gave money away usually to temples, churches or other places of worship, or helped the poor to show gratitude for their good fortune.

To feel better about being rich in a world where 80% of the populations live on less than $10 a day, make it a habit to donate some of your earnings to charity of your choice. Or, help someone you know is in need of financial support. Sharing helps money flow more easily.

9. Visualization

Daydreaming may be considered childish, but it is actually a way to charge your intention.

Imagine yourself as a wealthy person (regardless of what you see as wealth). Think about all the positive changes the wealth would bring to your life. Think who you would share it with. Think how you would make it grow. This way of thinking is influencing your subconscious to start feeling as if you are already rich. Feeling rich increases your chances of attracting real wealth.

10. Gratitude.

Don't forget to say THANK YOU at the end of each day. Be grateful for whatever you already have, even if it's much less than you think you deserve.

Saying thank you, and meaning it, brings grace to our lives and automatically raises our vibrations. This is very important as the law of attraction is all about positive energy.

Chapter 4:

Attracting Health

Unbeknown to us, our thoughts work all the time, which is quite scary when you come to think about it. Our health is a direct reflection of our mindset and the state of our health today is the result of the thoughts and beliefs we held in the past.

Changing our mindset takes time and lot of mental discipline, but the good news is that at least we can change the thoughts we have now, so as to improve our health in the future.

Manifesting the law of attraction for health improvement can be done preventively or reactively. In either case, BELEIVING that you can be cured is what seems to trigger the law of attraction.

For, just like there is the *placebo* effect (the power to heal, if positive thinking prevails), there is also the *nocebo* effect (the power NOT to heal, if negative thinking prevails). This means that

Chapter 4 - Attracting Health

the power to heal, or not to heal, ultimately lies with you, i.e. with the kind of thoughts you have.

There is no simple explanation how *placebo* effect contributes to healing, but, if we acknowledge that faith and expectation cause very real biochemical changes in the body, and positive thoughts are very much part and parcel of *placebo* effect, it becomes easier to understand how we can heal ourselves using mind-power.

Focusing on your intention and putting a lot of energy behind it is important for it to manifest, but bear in mind that sometimes wanting something very badly, actually stops you from having it.

When sending out an intention to the universe, send it with passion, but without urging desperation, for it seems that an intention sent out in fear or extreme anxiety, goes against the law of attraction principles. No matter how serious your condition may be, stay calm and focused and the universe will respond.

Here are 7 tips on how to help your health intentions manifest:

1. **De-stress**

    Chronic stress disrupts nearly every system in your body. It can raise blood pressure, suppress the immune system, increase the risk of heart attack and stroke, contribute to infertility, and speed up the aging process

    Before beginning health manifestations, try to learn stress management techniques. It is all about taking charge of your thoughts, your emotions, your environment, and the way you deal with problems. Learn how to change your reaction to stress and how to always make time for rest and relaxation.

    De-stressed and relaxed and you will be able to put in more energy behind your intention.

2. **Set intention**

    <u>Be specific</u> – are you trying to make a decision on how to proceed with your illness, or are you trying to lose/gain weight, or are you trying to find out what's

wrong with you? Rather than generalize (e.g. I'd like to stay healthy) focus on the specific health issue you want to address. Be fully aware of what you are trying to manifest with this intention.

<u>Be direct</u> – hit the nail on the head, spell out what's bothering you. If you can't say it, write it on a piece of paper which you will later burn and throw away.

<u>Be passionate</u> – put energy behind your intention. Visualize yourself as healthy, happy and strong. Feel the joy of being alive and confidence that you will be healed.

3. **Have faith**

It is scientifically proven that *placebo* effect works, so your thoughts should reflect your firm belief that you WILL get better. Wish with all your heart to get well, without allowing yourself to ever get desperate or doubtful. Desperation and doubt (in your voice or thoughts) will weaken the power of intention.

4. Your environment

If faced with a serious health problem, you need to create an environment of support and reflection, in which you can become receptive to your innate healing powers. You need to be somewhere where you feel absolutely safe.

If you share your home with someone, you need to create a private space where you will recuperate and where furniture or room decoration will reflect your intention to get better. Add flowers, crystals, photographs, various small things which remind you of happier times and make you feel good and relaxed.

However, if you feel that your home, or home environment (family members, room-mates, neighbors) are a constant source of stress, anxiety and negativity, you need to get out of there as soon as you can. Sometimes, the only thing it takes to move from a negative to a positive mindset is a change of scene.

Chapter 4 - Attracting Health

5. **Affirmations**

   Affirmations are crucial if you are trying to manifest with the law of attraction. They stop you from forgetting what your goals are. You can copy some ideas for affirmations that others are using, but the best thing is to coin an affirmation which comes from your heart. Say out loud what you would really like to happen (even if, at the moment, it sounds highly unlikely), then keep on repeating it throughout the day. Believe in the words you are saying.

6. **Don't stay at home**

   Unless your illness is such that you have to stay in bed, continue going to work, doing your hobbies, seeing the people you normally socialize with. There is something about being at home, in a dressing gown, surrounded by medication and cups of tea that really undermines one's energy. When ill, you need to boost your immune system rather than sabotage it.

7. Connect With Positive People

If you have a health problem, now more than ever you need to choose your company carefully. Stay away from those who make you feel uncomfortable or who, somehow, undermine your confidence and self-worth. Even close friends are not always well-meaning. When you are ill, you need all the positive energy you can muster, so preserve your energy by surrounding yourself with people in whose company you feel loved and loving, who make you feel good about yourself.

Don't isolate yourself from the world, but if protecting yourself from draining or negative energy means being on your own for a while, even that is better than having to endure patronizing false concerns.

Chapter 5:

The Ultimate Goal: Abundance and Happiness

Abundance

Have you ever asked yourself how to manifest abundance in your life? Almost everyone has.

However, abundance means different things to different people. To most, it represents money and wealth, but abundance can manifest in many other ways, such as love, family, health and vitality, etc.

Before trying to manifest abundance, ask yourself what is your idea of an abundant life. What is it that you really want? Money, big family, career, stability, adventure, peace? Only then will you know when, and if, it has actually manifested.

Chapter 5 - The Ultimate Goal: Abundance and Happiness

To manifest abundance, you have to develop a mindset which supports the feeling of "plenty" rather than the feeling of "lack".

Many of us were brought up with the notion that life is hard. Even the Bible says "Who said life was easy"? Those who agree with this kind of thinking automatically accept that it's normal to struggle through life, to always lack something, to never have enough of what you need. These people live their lives with the "lack" mentality.

Living in an abundant way means you are less anxious about the future and less fearful of unexpected chain of events. Living a life of abundance means being happy with whom you are and with the way your life is unfolding. With this kind of positive thinking you also shield yourself from negative energy which often surrounds us.

Abundance manifests easily if it becomes a way of life. To invite abundance into your life, you have to accept that the most important thing about abundance is attitude and your attitude is something you CAN learn to control.

Here are 4 steps on how to invite abundance into your life:

1. Try spreading abundance to all aspects of your life - relationships, family, friends, career, and money. True abundance comes when you have balance in your life.

2. Live a life that makes your heart full, knowing you are living the way you want to, and you feel deep down that you are doing the right thing.

3. Changing your mindset will also change your life. Think out of the box, think with hope in your heart and opportunities will start presenting themselves. Life somehow seems to flow more smoothly when there is harmony.

4. Abundance can't manifest without self-love. You have to believe that you deserve what you want and that you will get it. This way of thinking will make your personal energy field radiate positive energy and that will raise your vibrations. With raised vibrations you are much more likely to attract from the universe whatever you need.

Chapter 5 - The Ultimate Goal: Abundance and Happiness

Happiness

A positive mindset is crucial if you want more happiness in your life. No one is born happy, or unhappy, but we have to constantly strive to create circumstances which will attract happiness into our life.

These are 4 basic actions to take to improve your overall chance of happiness:

1. **Take responsibility for your life**

    The life we live now is the result of the thoughts we had in the past. But, if you feel you are paying dearly for the bad decisions you once made, do not despair because even though your present may be far from agreeable, your actions of today can, and will, shape your future. The trouble is, bad life choices tend to have a domino effect, and one wrong decision often leads to another. When we are young, we don't fully grasp the enormity of responsibility our actions have for our future. With every choice you make, e.g. choice of a partner, choice of profession, choice of people you hang around with, you are actually writing a chapter of your life.

2. Protect your aura

Avoid situations, places and people who you know, or suspect, will make you feel uncomfortable. Our physical health is directly linked to the health of our energy field. Strong and resilient aura helps us maintain good health, emotional stability and spiritual growth.

3. Build Self-esteem

Self-esteem is about being proud of yourself and who you are. Not being full of yourself, just happy with where you are in life right now. Self-esteem comes from positive self-image and needs to be nurtured.

4. Enjoy life

For a start, find what "turns you on" and then do it as often as you can. Doing things we enjoy or being with people we feel good around makes a big difference in the quality of our life.

Chapter 5 - The Ultimate Goal: Abundance and Happiness

> Try to live the life that suits you. Don't blindly follow the latest trend, rather find your own niche and build your life around it. This applies to both your career and the lifestyle you choose for yourself.
>
> Use your strengths to become really good at what you do best. Match your personality to your career, or even better, do something you feel passionate about.
>
> Although it might be very tempting, never choose a career based only on its earning potential, because in the long run, only doing what you're passionate about creates work-life balance that makes life worth living.
>
> And most importantly, try to enjoy your life NOW without waiting for something big in the future.

Abundance and happiness go hand-in-hand with self-love and faith. As Deepak Chopra so beautifully put it, "Abundance is when you experience joy, health, happiness, sense of purpose and vitality".

Closing

The power of repeated thoughts and words is unbelievable. Everything we say, or think, has the potential to either heal or harm. Use words carefully when you speak to others, but be even more careful when you speak to, or about, yourself.

Words and thoughts can be harnessed both for positive manifestation, as well as for undermining others, or oneself. Practice positive self-talk and you will start to experience the difference to how you feel.

If you can't motivate yourself to feel positive about your life, start using affirmations. They are positive words that can boost your confidence and transform your life by causing your subconscious mind to accept as true what you keep saying. That way, words can attract corresponding events and situations into your life.

Don't suppress your feelings, particularly your gut feelings. Connect to your inner self, i.e. to

Closing

your intuitive nature. That helps tap into the abundance the universe offers to anyone who cares to open their mind and listen.

Thank you again for purchasing this book!

I hope this book was able to help you to understand more about the law of attraction and how to manifest the enriching life you deserve!

The next step is to go and apply what you learned in this book!

Finally, if you enjoyed this book, then I'd like to ask you for a favor, would you be kind enough to leave a review for this book? It'd be greatly appreciated!

Thank you and good luck!

www.ingramcontent.com/pod-product-compliance
Lightning Source LLC
Chambersburg PA
CBHW052106110526
44591CB00013B/2378